AF413255

Nyla's Check Adventure

Written by Sarha Simeon Wright

Written by Sarha Simeon Wright
Illustrated by C.Beyond Marketing Resource Center, LLC & TP Studios

ISBN 979-8-9902770-0-7 (hardcover)

First hardcover edition 2024

Published by Ayevol Holdings Group, LLC
www.nylascheckadventure.com.

This Book Belongs to

____

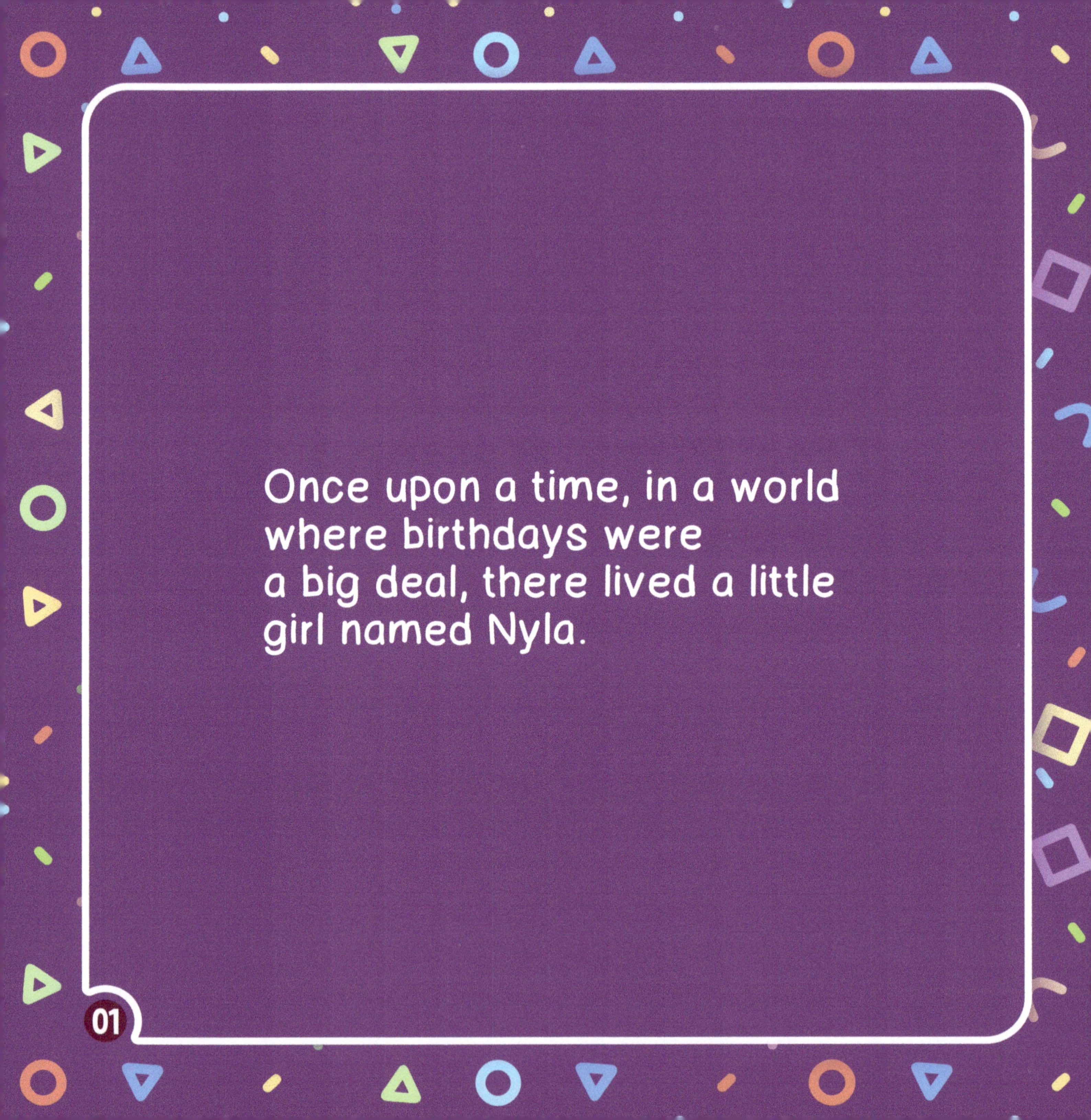

Once upon a time, in a world where birthdays were
a big deal, there lived a little girl named Nyla.

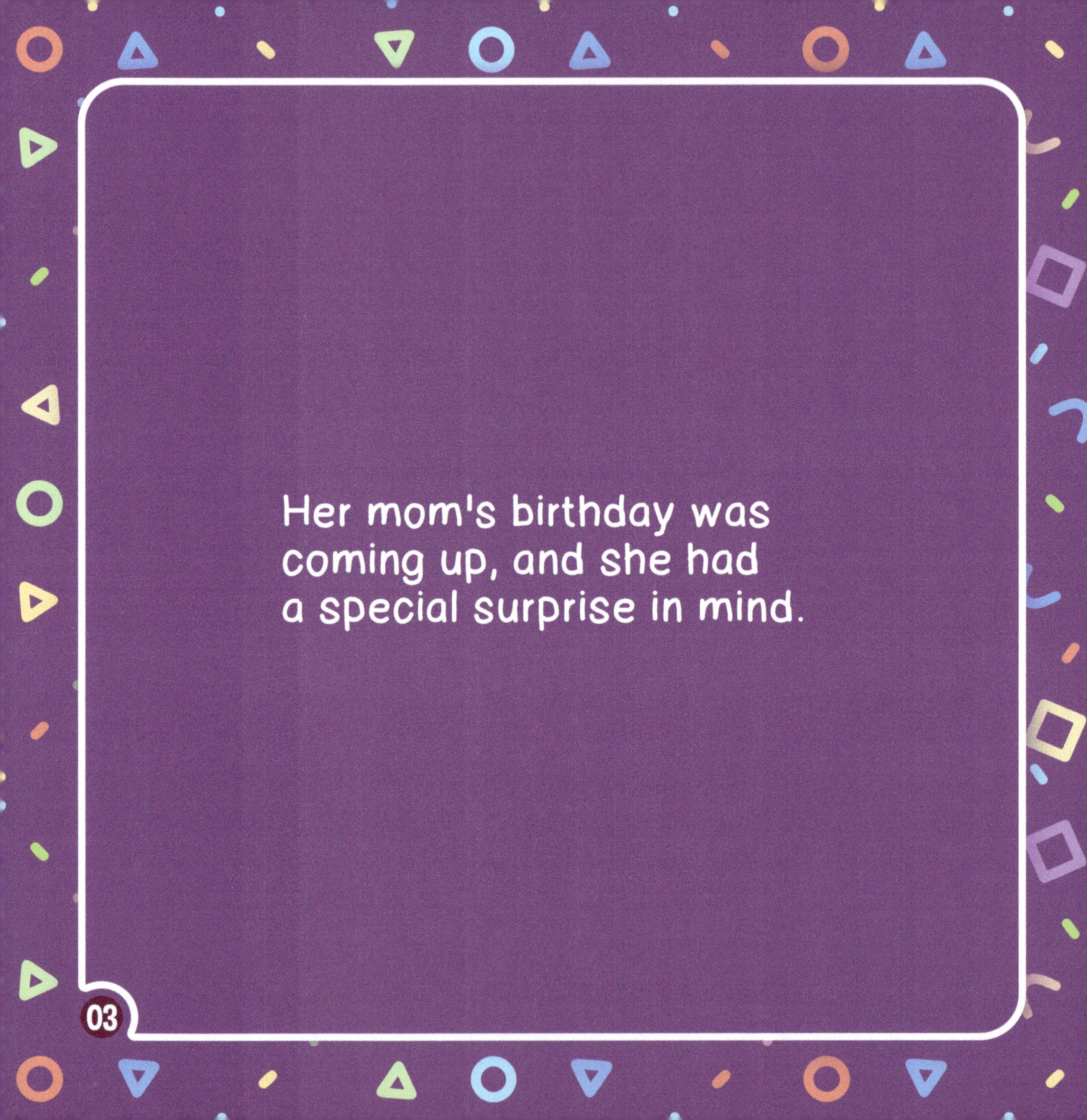
Her mom's birthday was
coming up, and she had
a special surprise in mind.
03

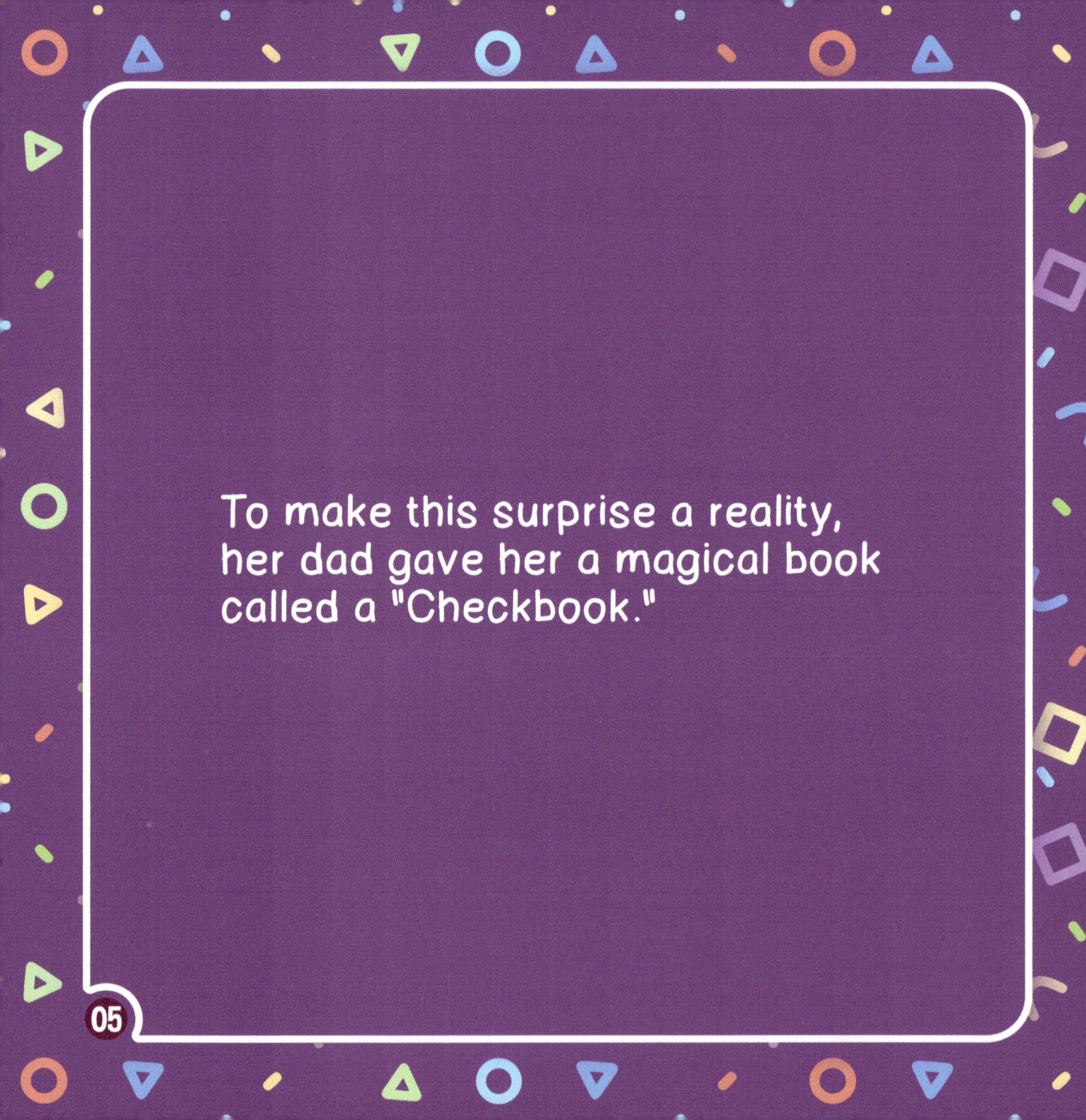
To make this surprise a reality,
her dad gave her a magical book
called a "Checkbook."

Blk Mlnre
Dear Diary
06

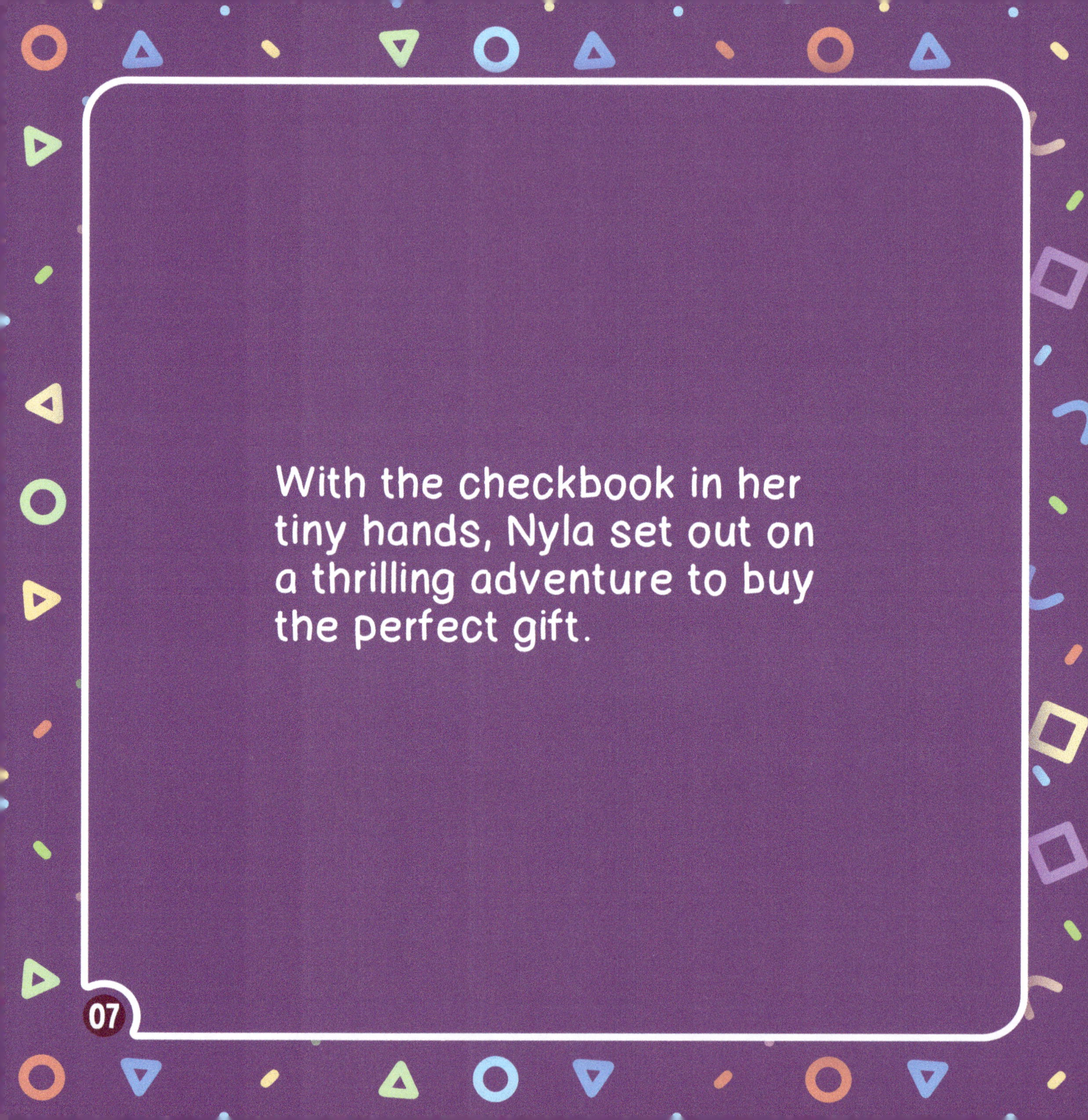

With the checkbook in her tiny hands, Nyla set out on a thrilling adventure to buy the perfect gift.

08

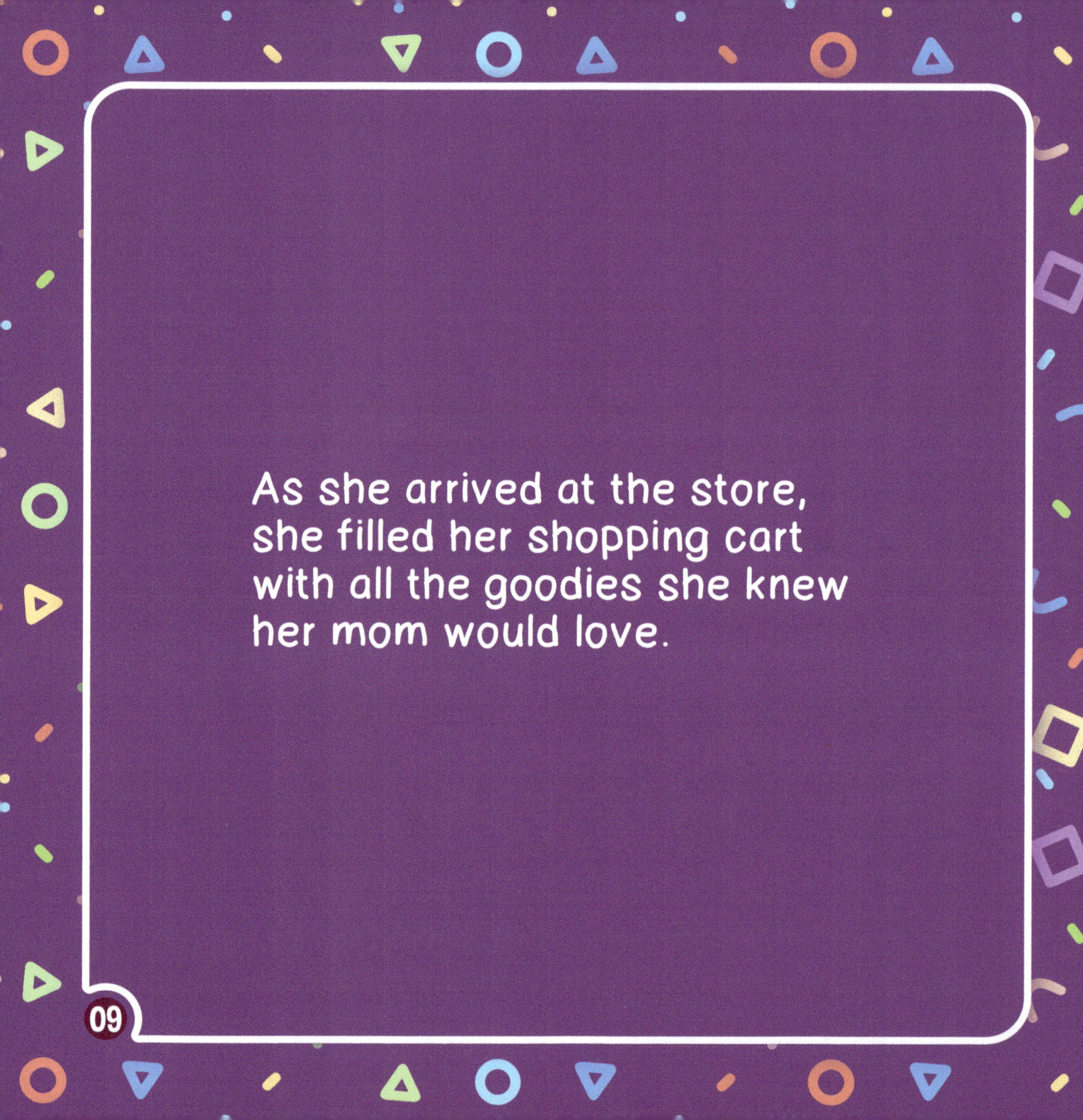

As she arrived at the store,
she filled her shopping cart
with all the goodies she knew
her mom would love.

10

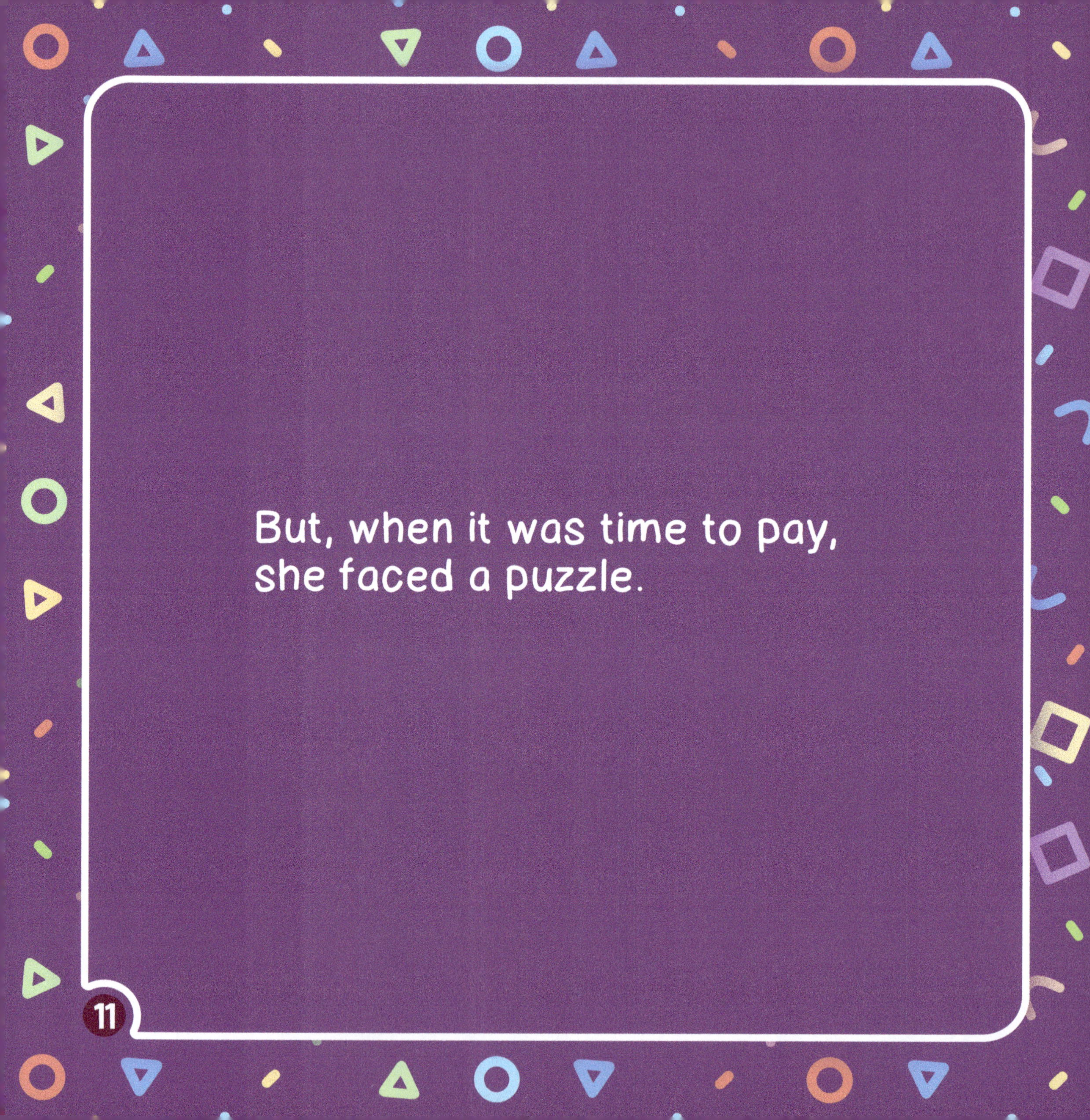

But, when it was time to pay,
she faced a puzzle.

75.99
12.99
SALE
50%
12

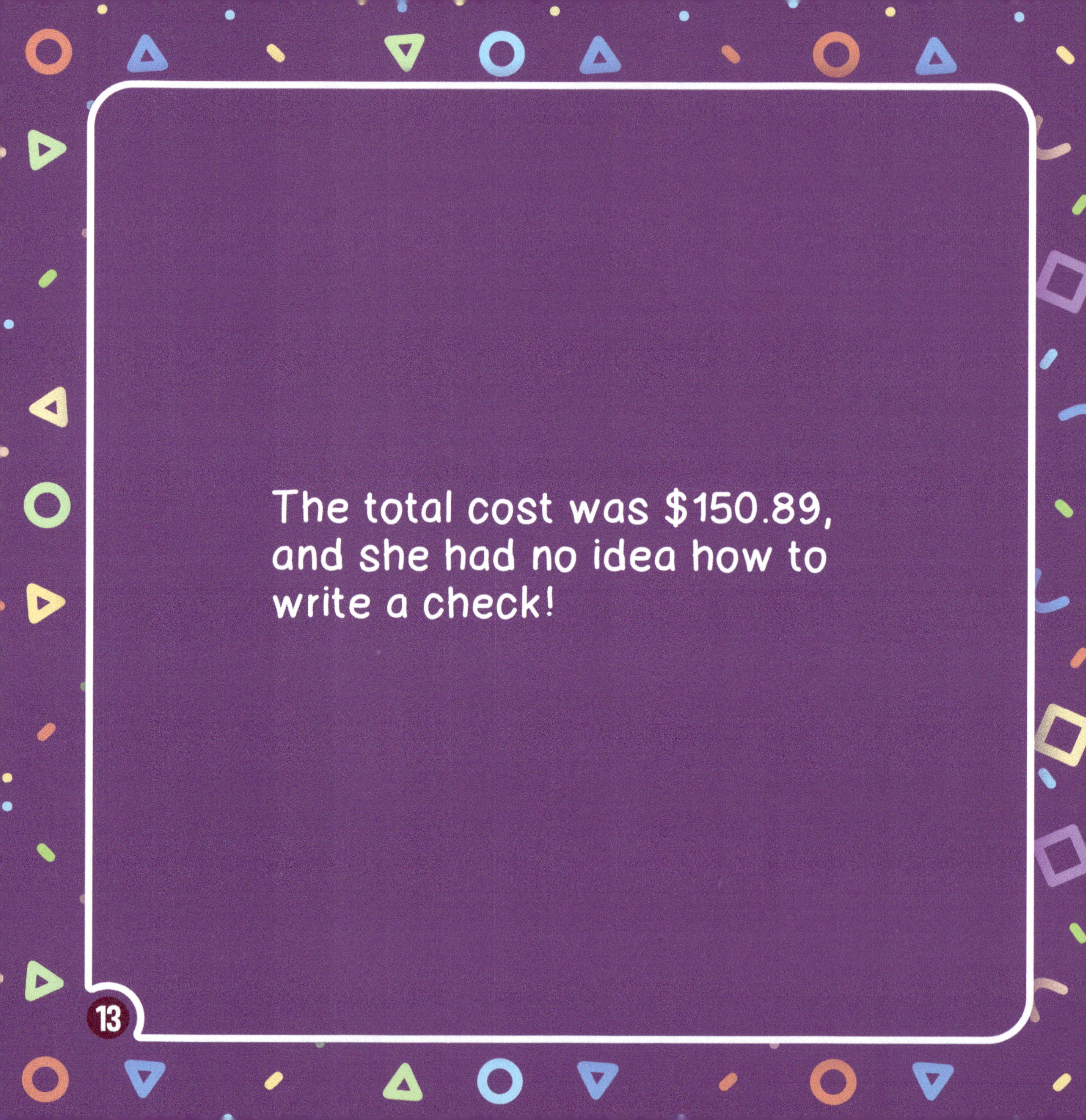
The total cost was $150.89, and she had no idea how to write a check!

SALE
50%
14

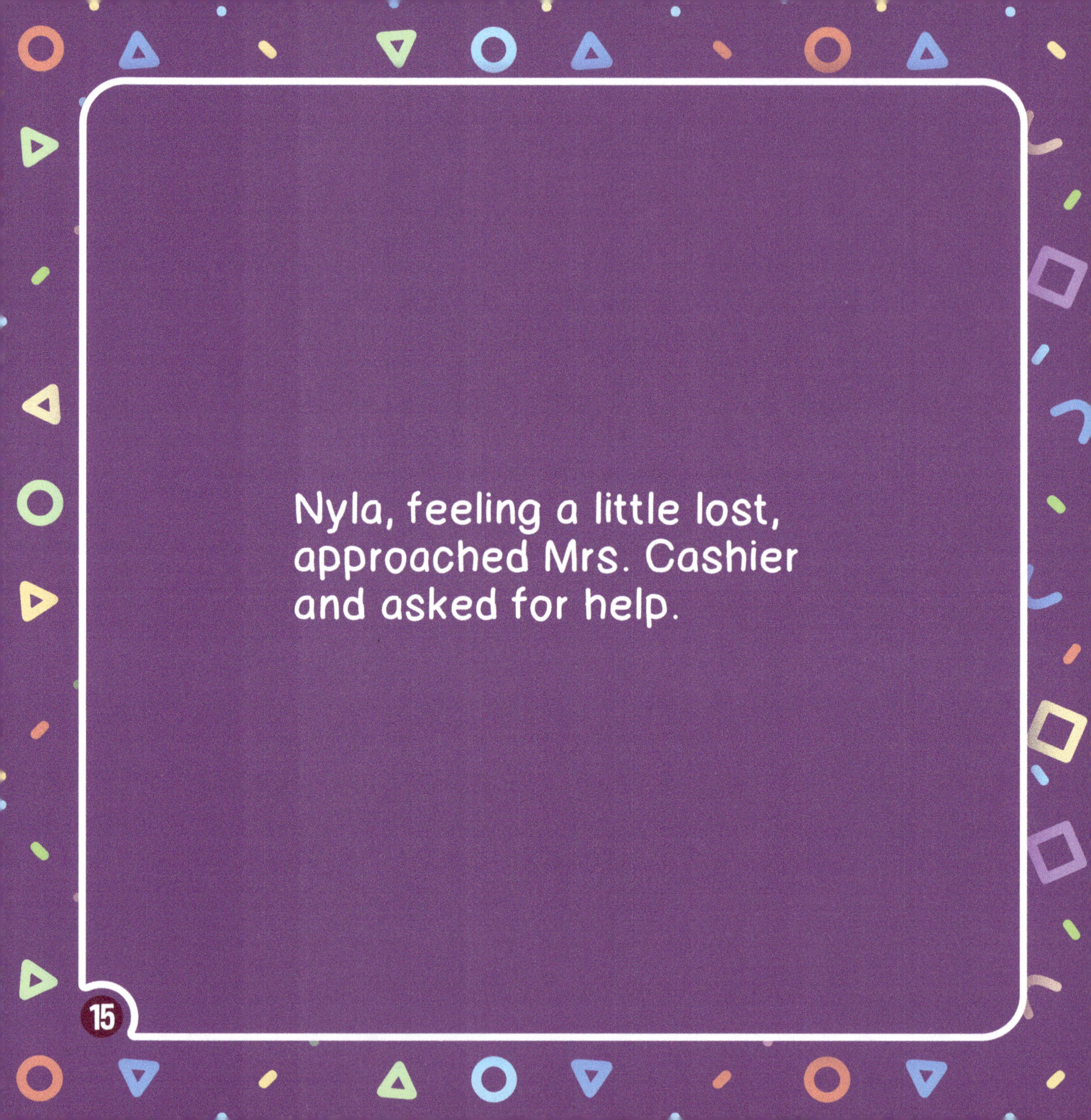
Nyla, feeling a little lost,
approached Mrs. Cashier
and asked for help.

16

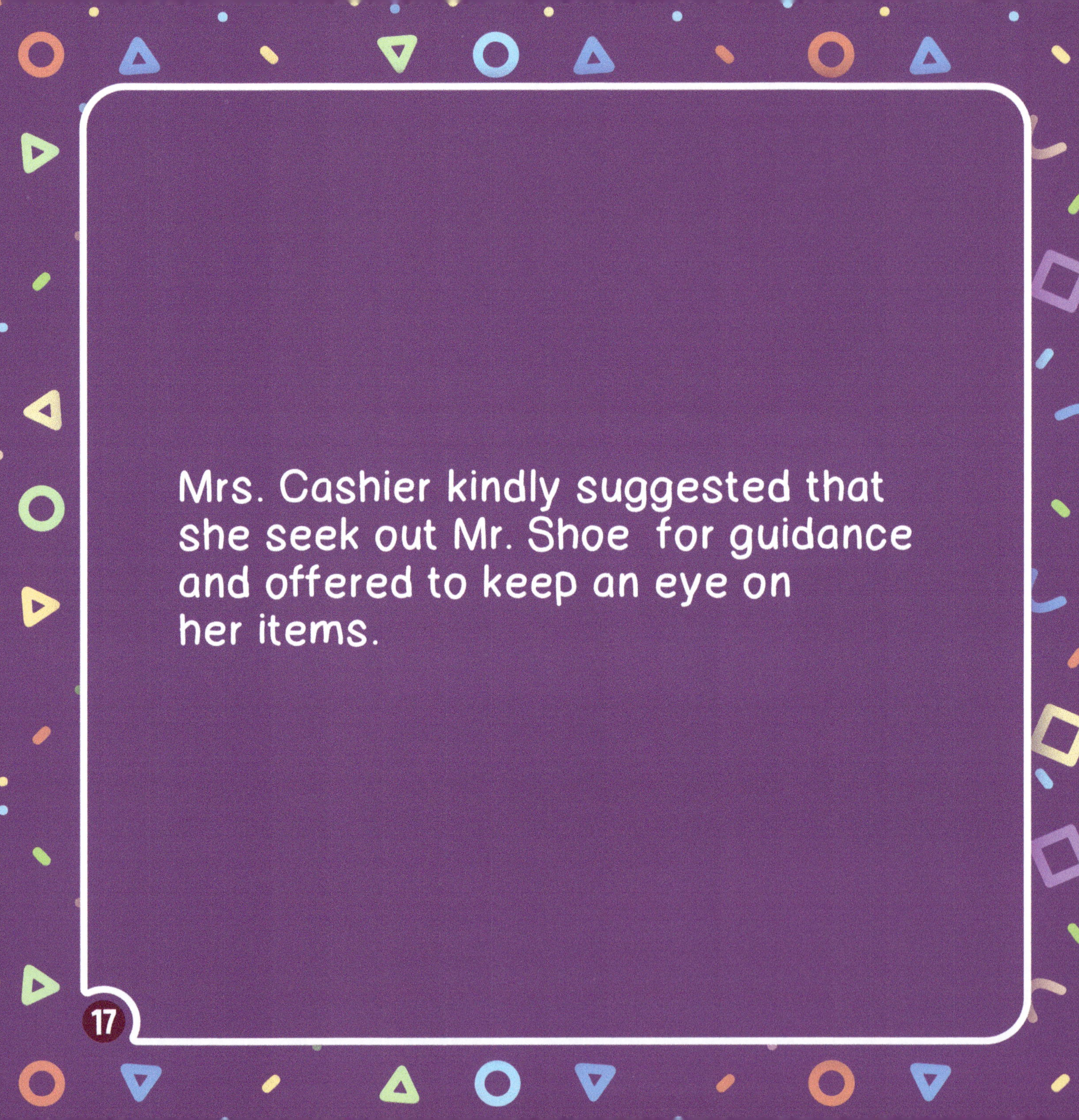
Mrs. Cashier kindly suggested that
she seek out Mr. Shoe for guidance
and offered to keep an eye on
her items.

Mr. Shoe

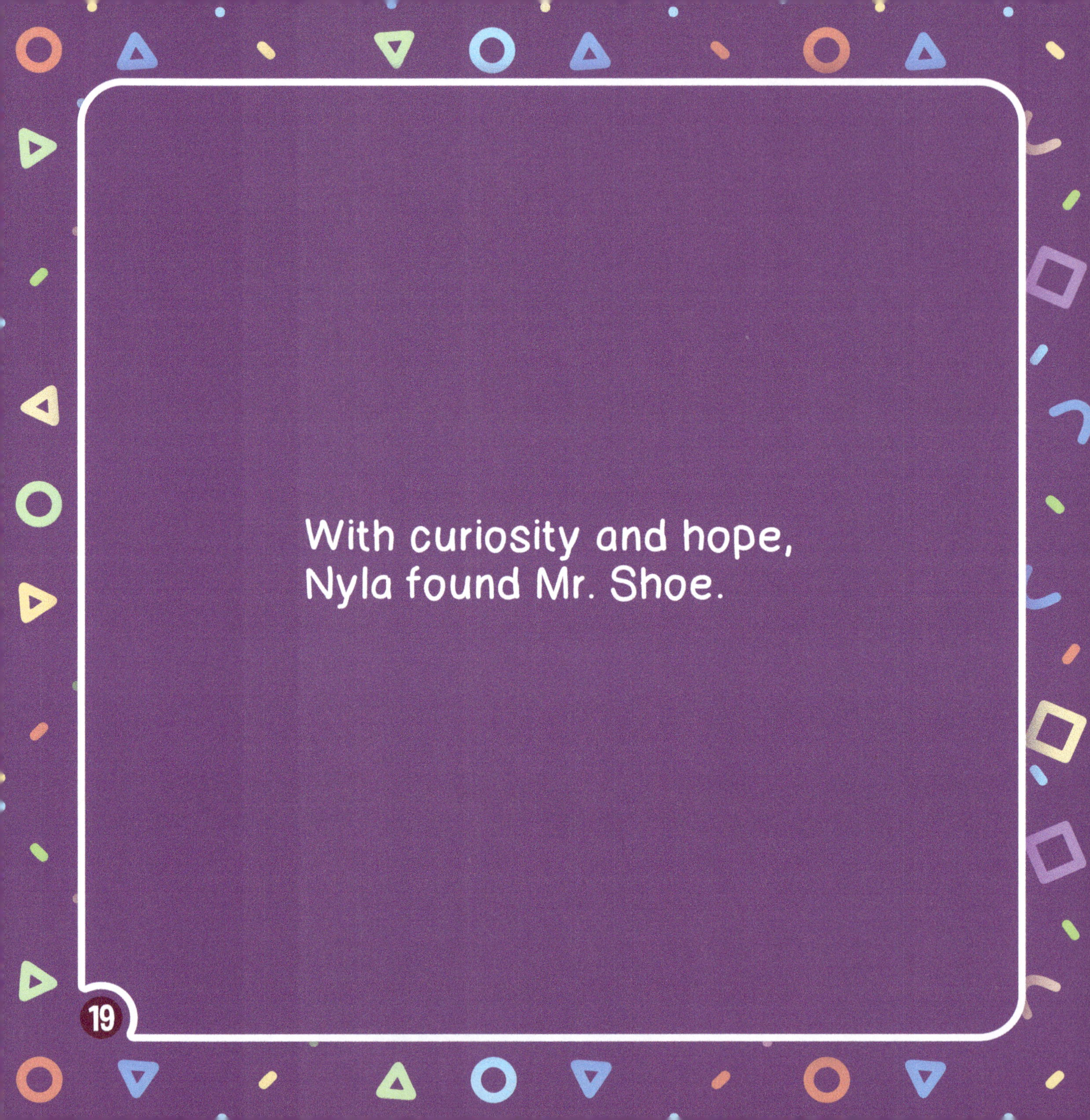

With curiosity and hope,
Nyla found Mr. Shoe.

20

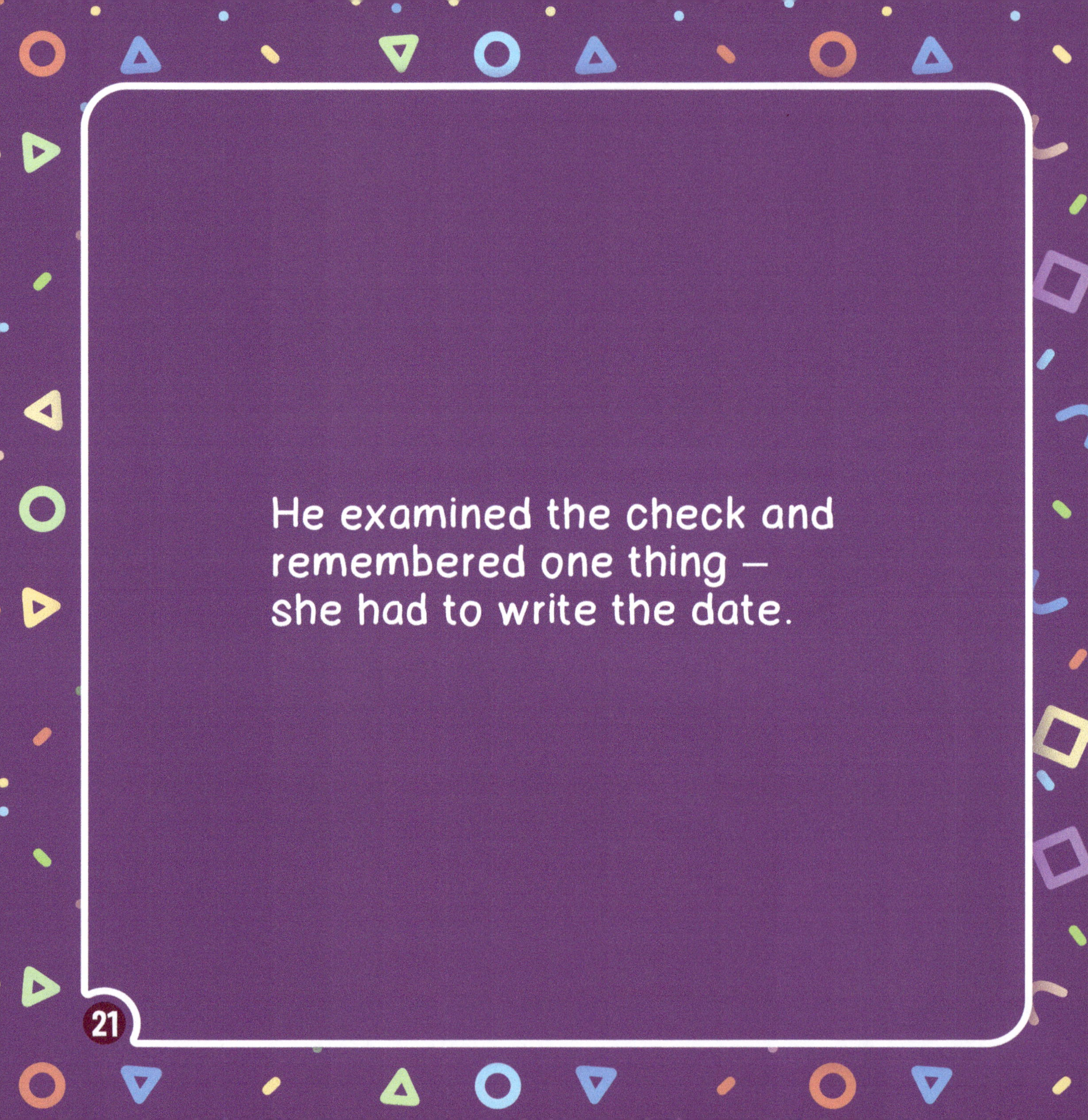

He examined the check and
remembered one thing —
she had to write the date.

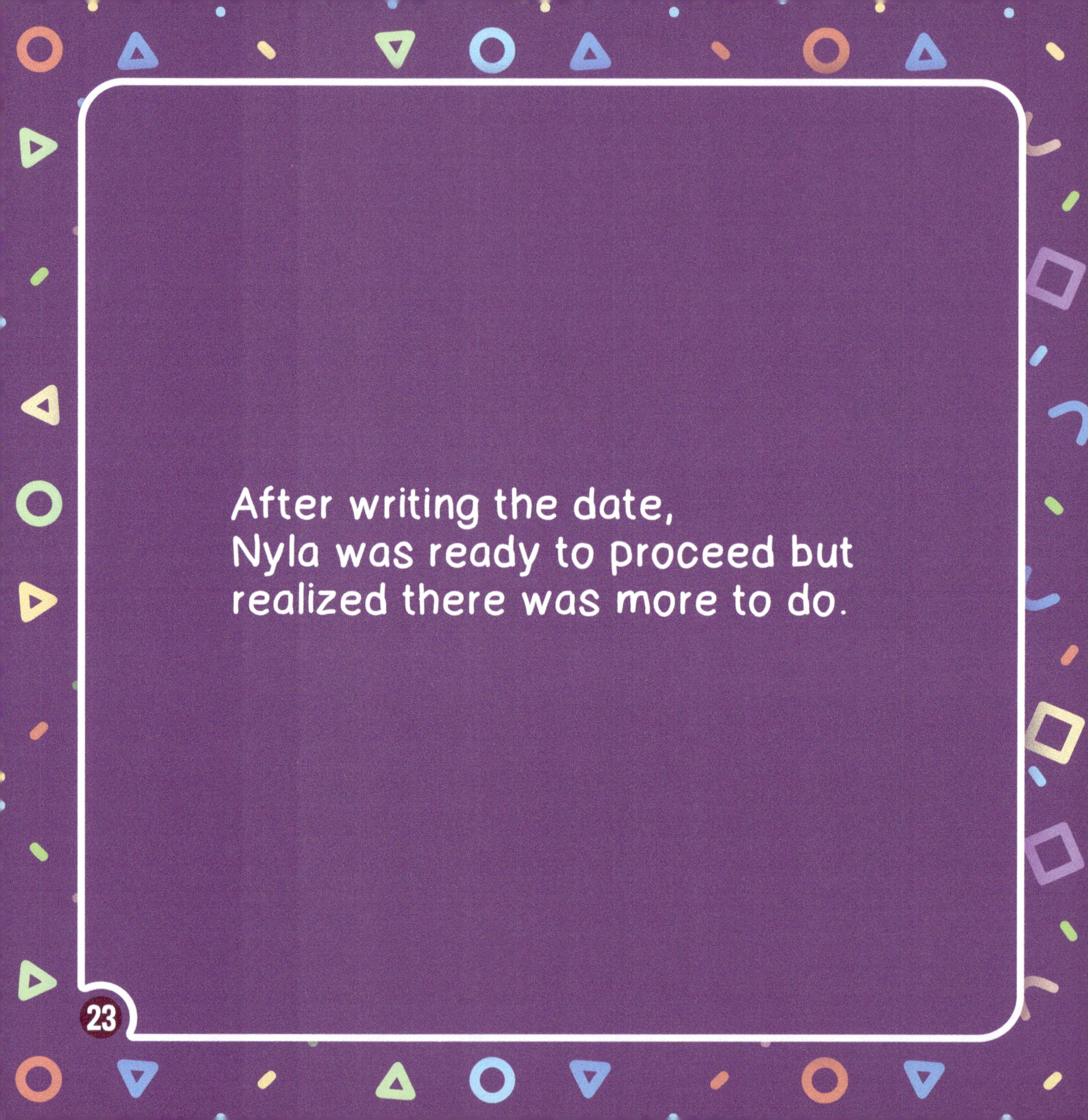

After writing the date,
Nyla was ready to proceed but
realized there was more to do.

Mr. Shoe

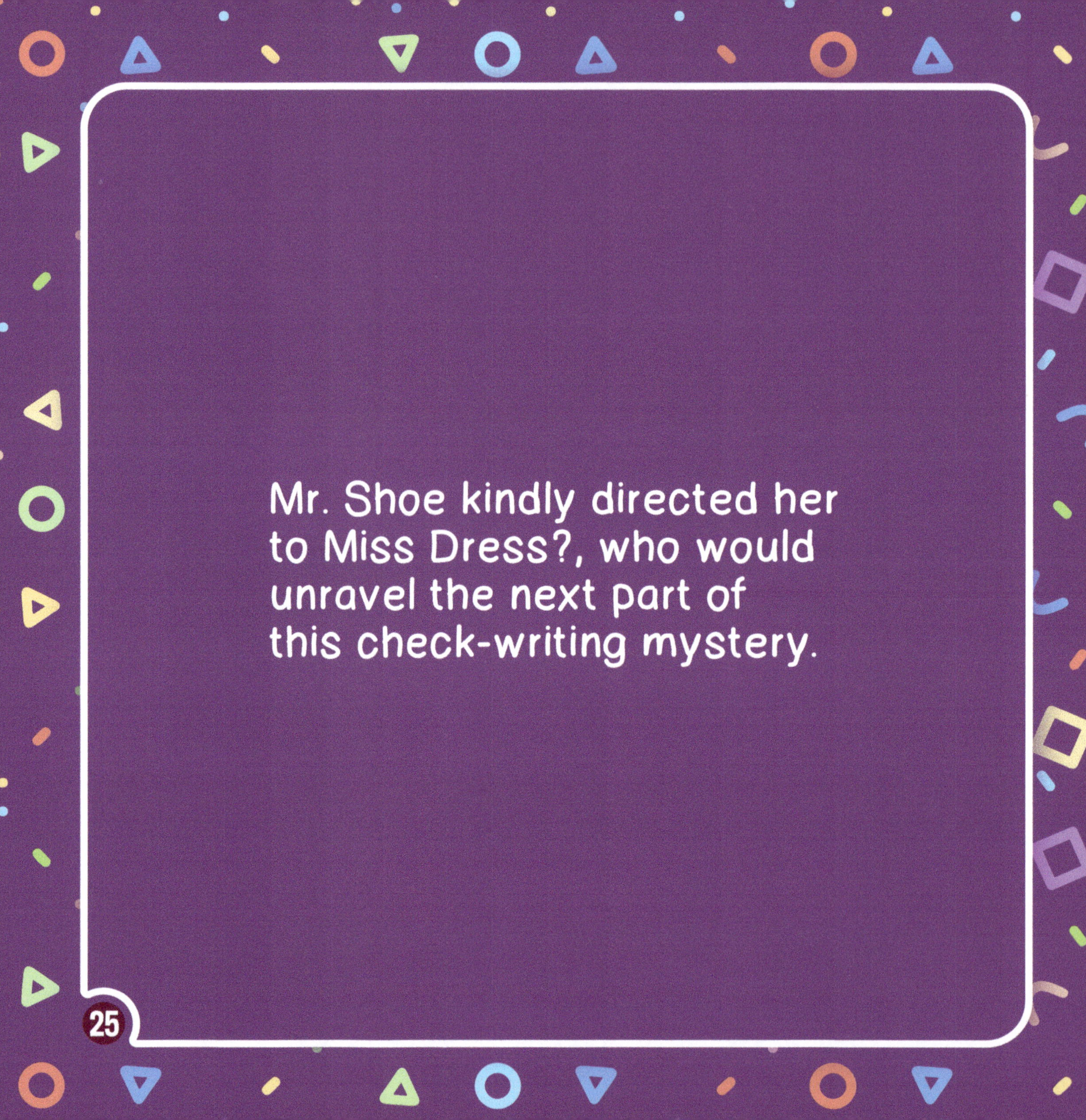
Mr. Shoe kindly directed her
to Miss Dress?, who would
unravel the next part of
this check-writing mystery.

26

Miss Dress looked at the check
and noticed Nyla had already
dated it correctly.

Nyla Minre
380 Wrightway Street
Wealth Builders, USA 18111
02/03/2024
Date
Pay To The
Order Of
$
Dollars
For

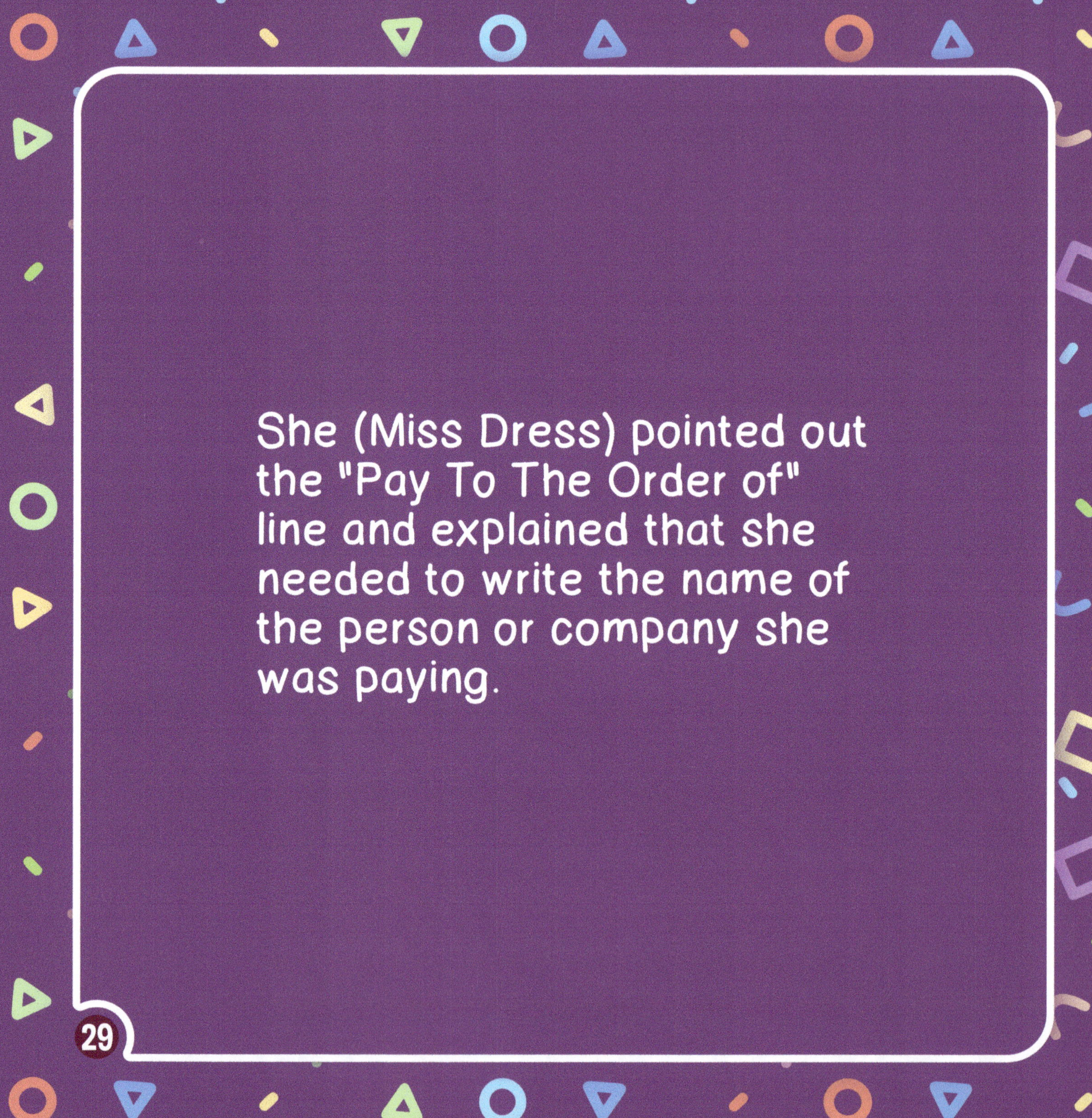

She (Miss Dress) pointed out the "Pay To The Order of" line and explained that she needed to write the name of the person or company she was paying.

Nyla Mlnre
360 Wrightway Street
Wealth Builders,USA 10111
Pay To The
Order Of   The Store
For
30

Nyla followed her advice, but Miss Dress couldn't recall the rest and suggested talking to Mr. Coat .

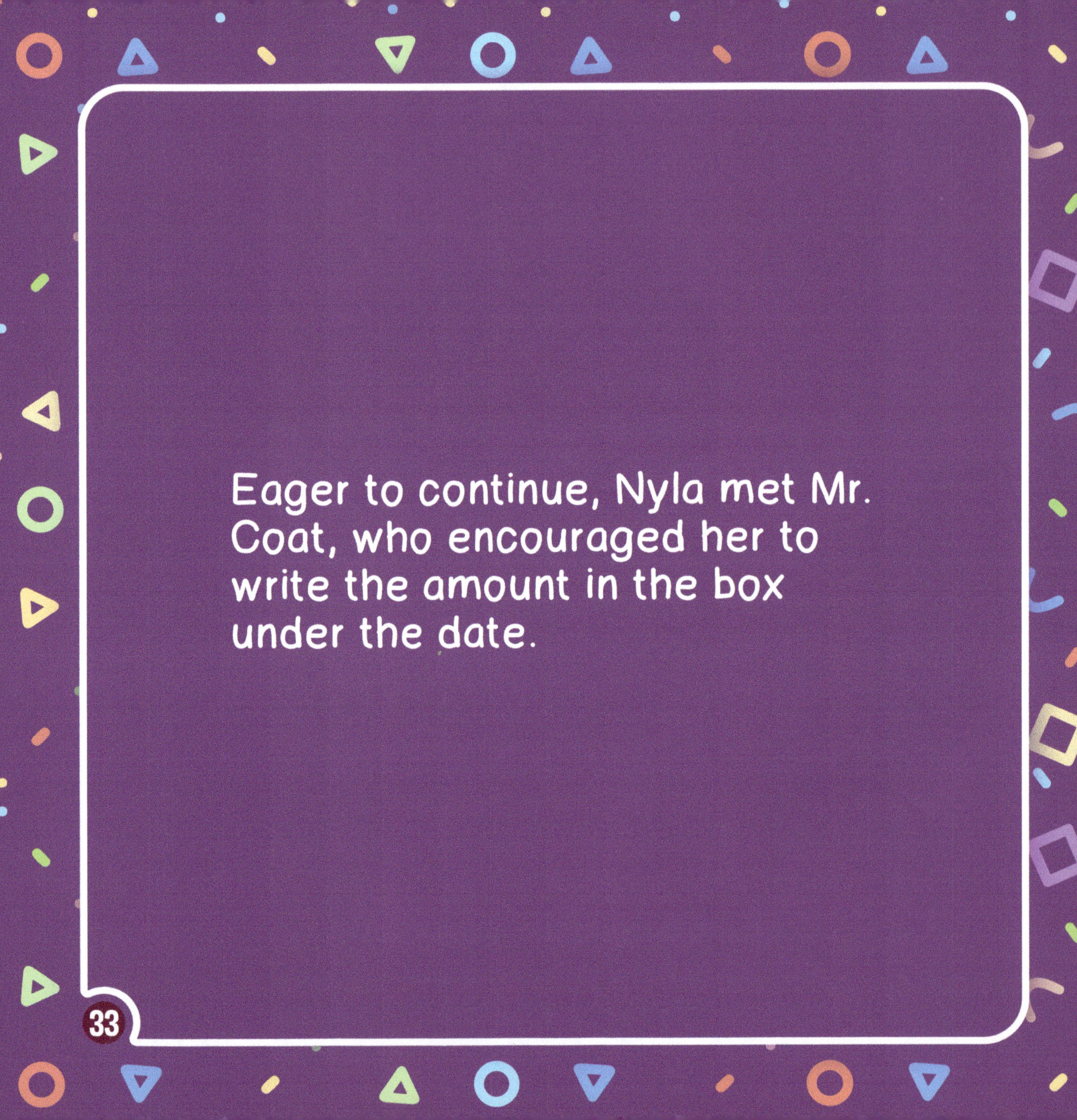

Eager to continue, Nyla met Mr. Coat, who encouraged her to write the amount in the box under the date.

34

With " $150.89" written, he admitted
he couldn't remember what came
next and suggested Mrs. Pants?.

tore
The Store
Pay To The
Order Of
For
36

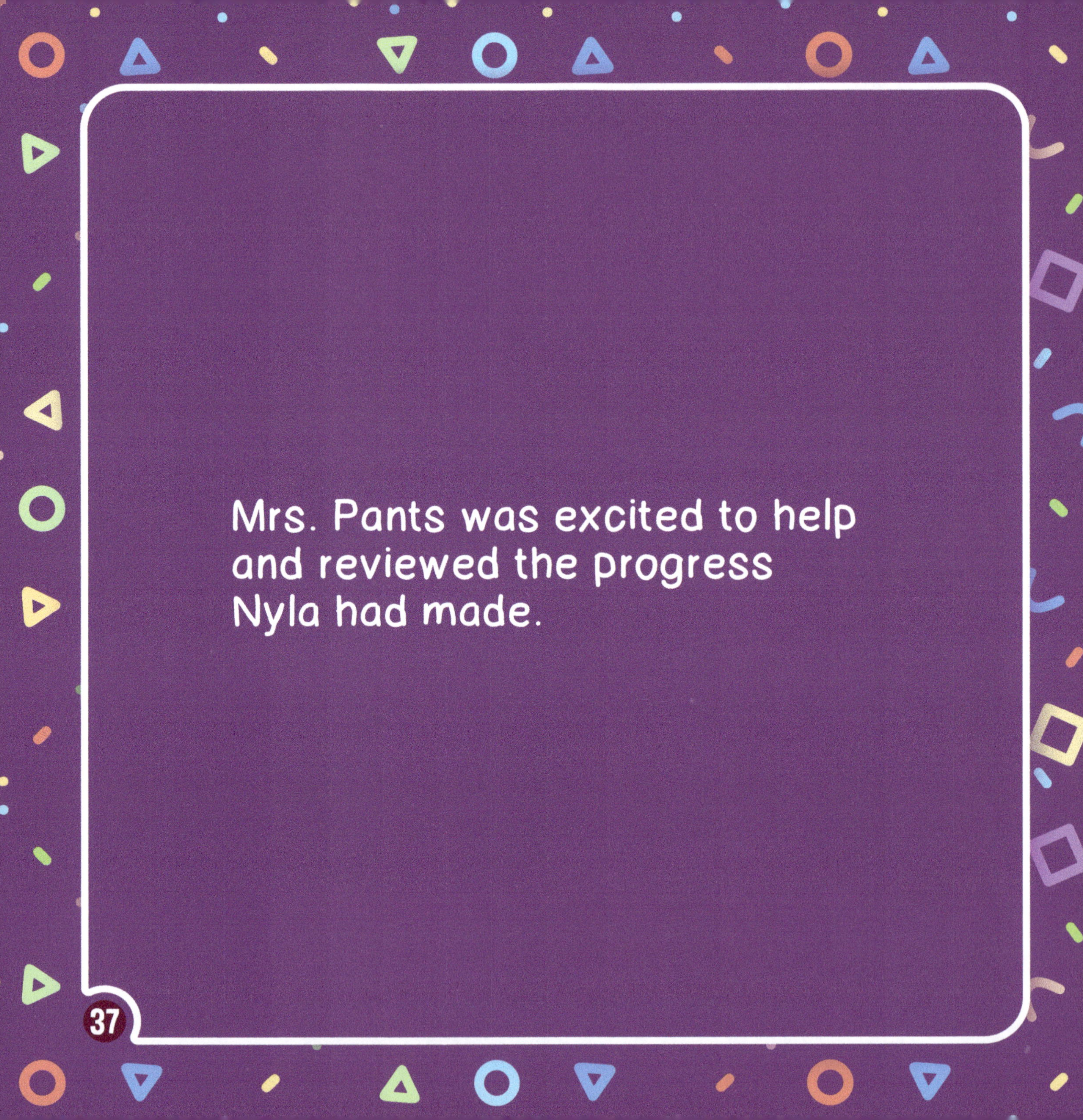
Mrs. Pants was excited to help
and reviewed the progress
Nyla had made.

Nyla Minre
360 Wrighway Street
Wealth Builders,USA 10111
1000
Date
02/05/2024
Pay To The The Store
Order Of
$ 150.89
Dollars
38

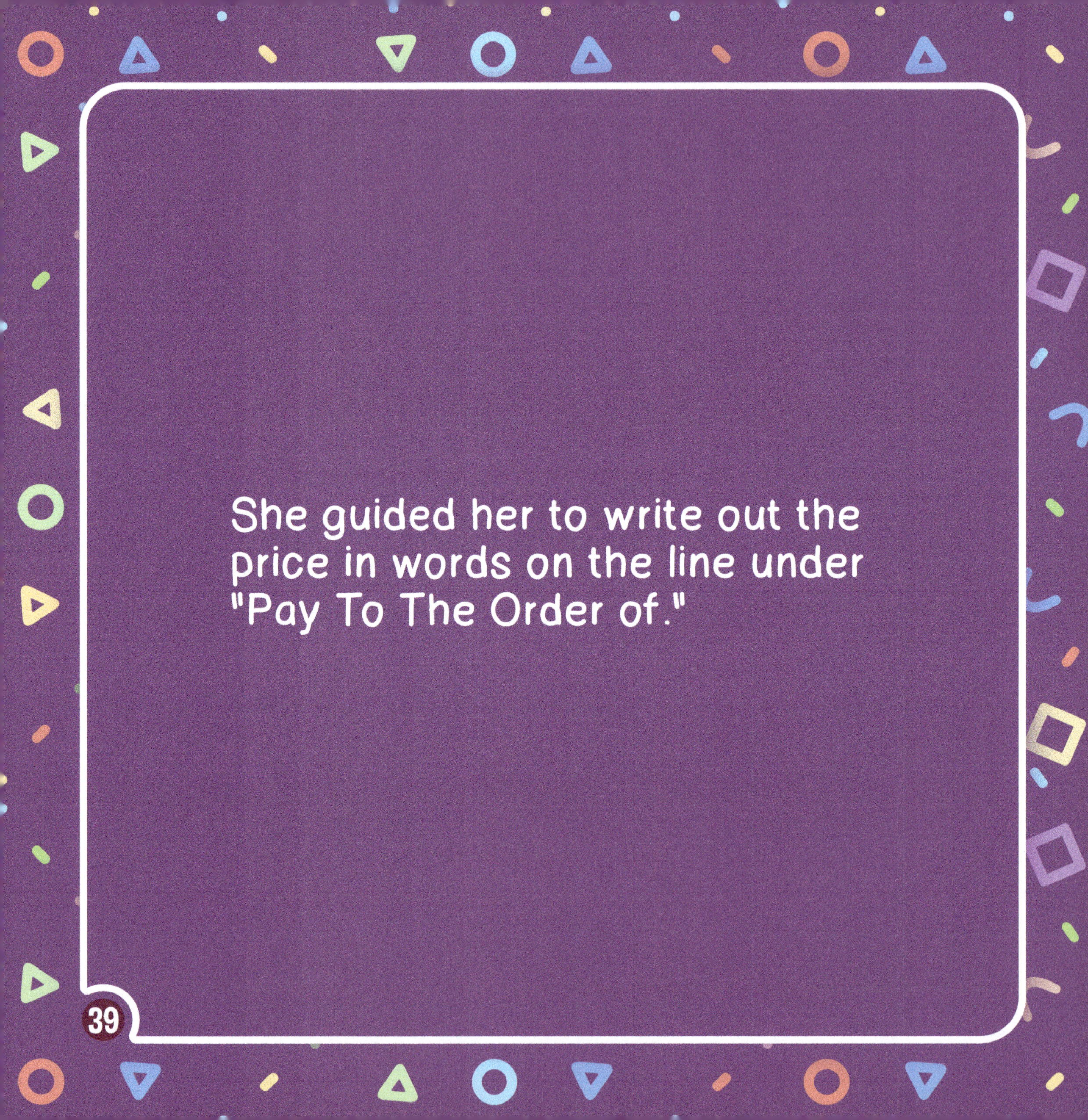

She guided her to write out the price in words on the line under "Pay To The Order of."

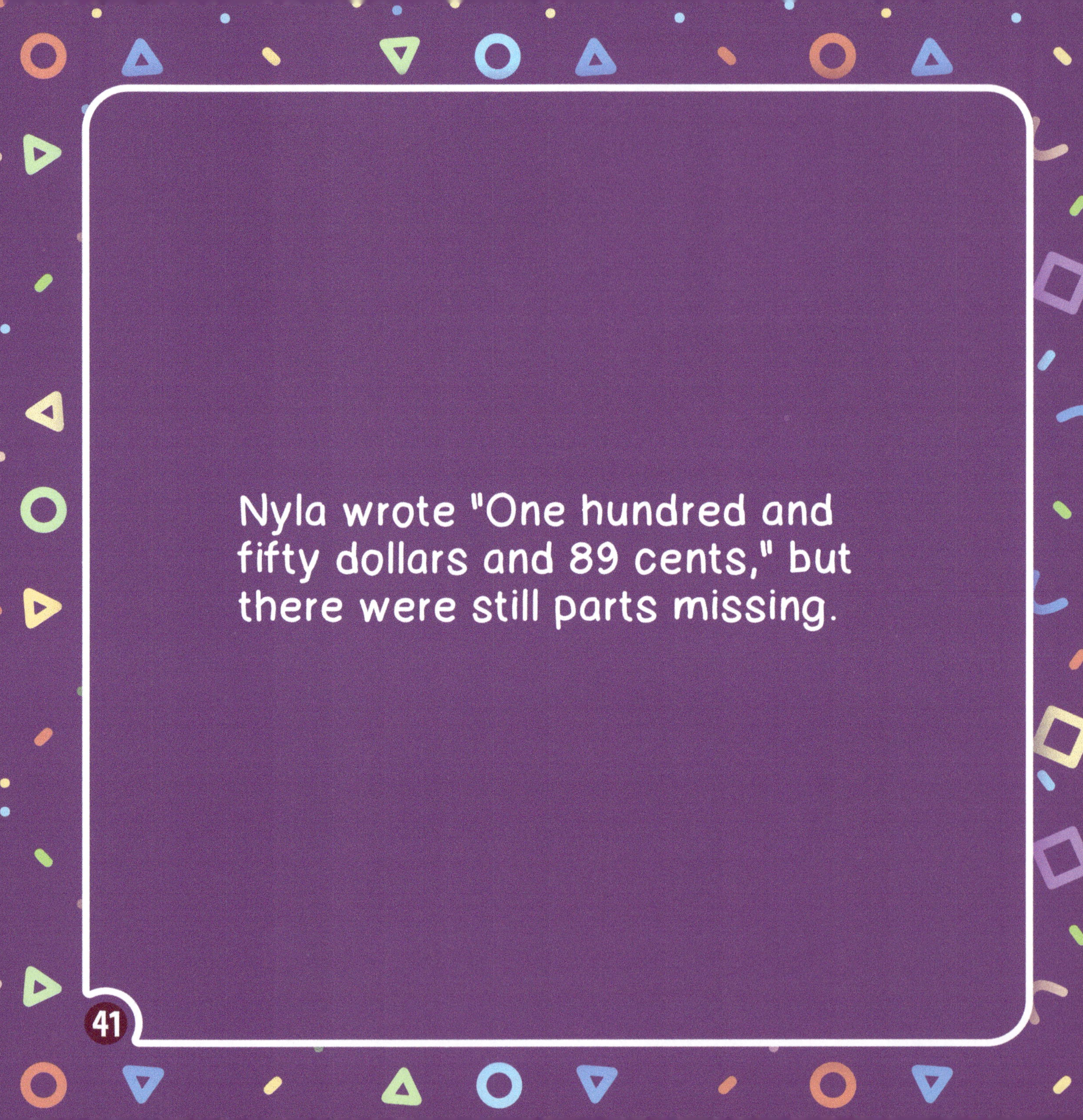

Nyla wrote "One hundred and fifty dollars and 89 cents," but there were still parts missing.

1000
Nyla MInre
360 Wrightway Street
Wealth Builders,USA 10111
02/05/2024
Date
$ 150.89
Pay To The Order Of   The Store
One Hundred & Fifty Dollars and Eighty Nine Cents   Dollars
For

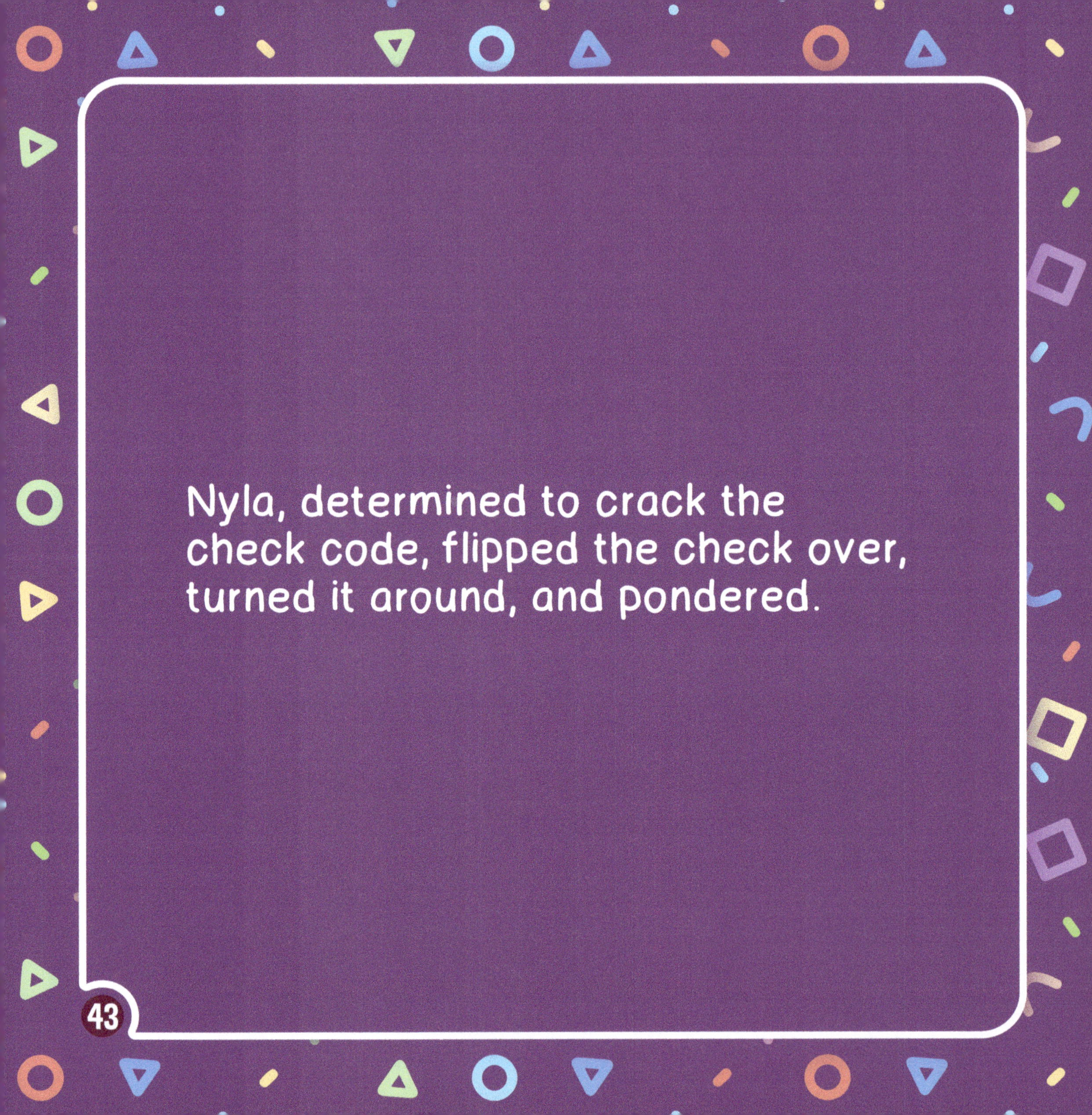

Nyla, determined to crack the check code, flipped the check over, turned it around, and pondered.

44

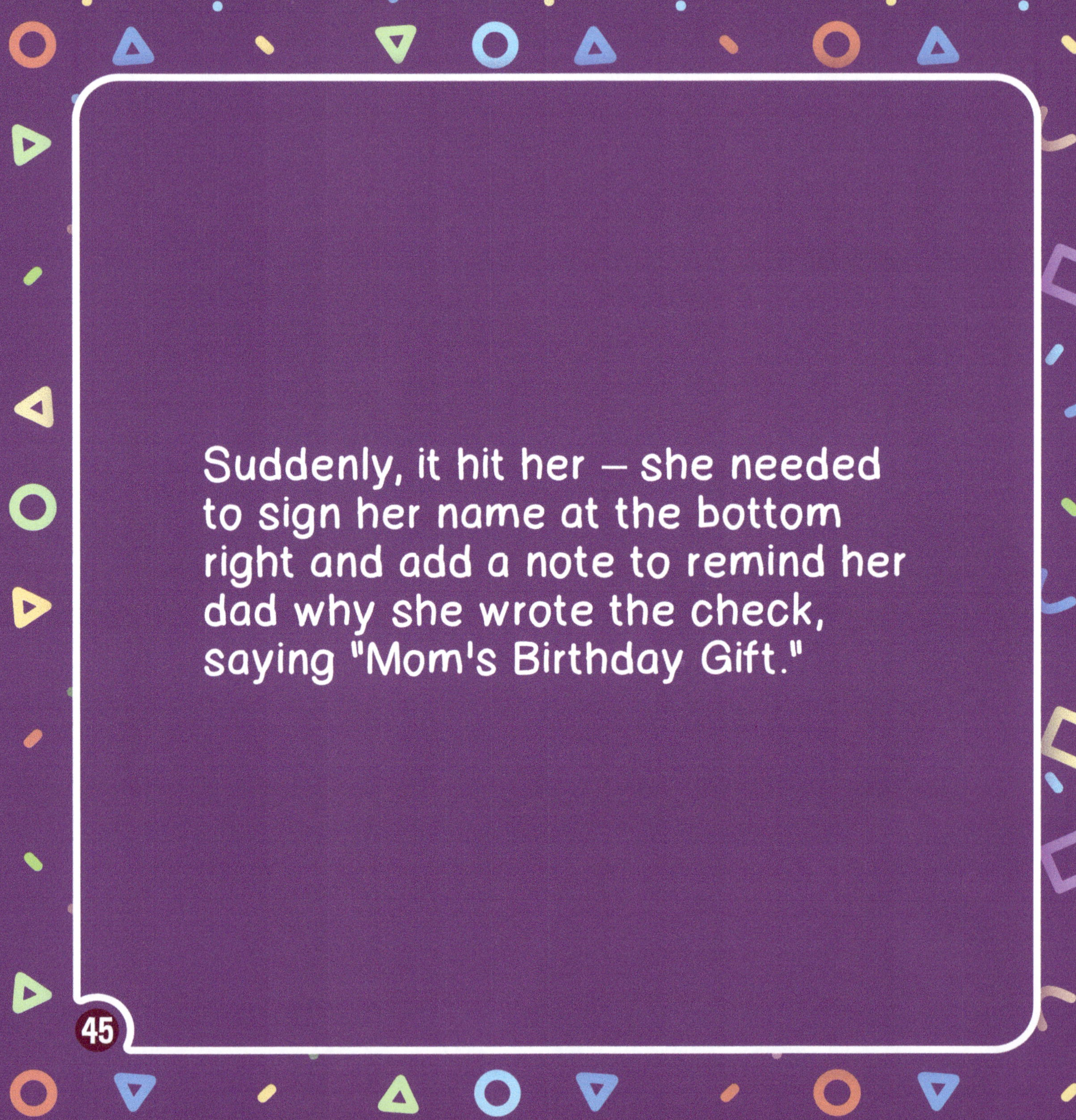
Suddenly, it hit her — she needed
to sign her name at the bottom
right and add a note to remind her
dad why she wrote the check,
saying "Mom's Birthday Gift."

MInre
Wrightway Street
th Builders,USA 10111
02/05/2024
Date
150.89
The Store
dred & Fifty Dollars and Eighty Nine Cents Dollars
Nyla MInre
Mom's Birthday Gift

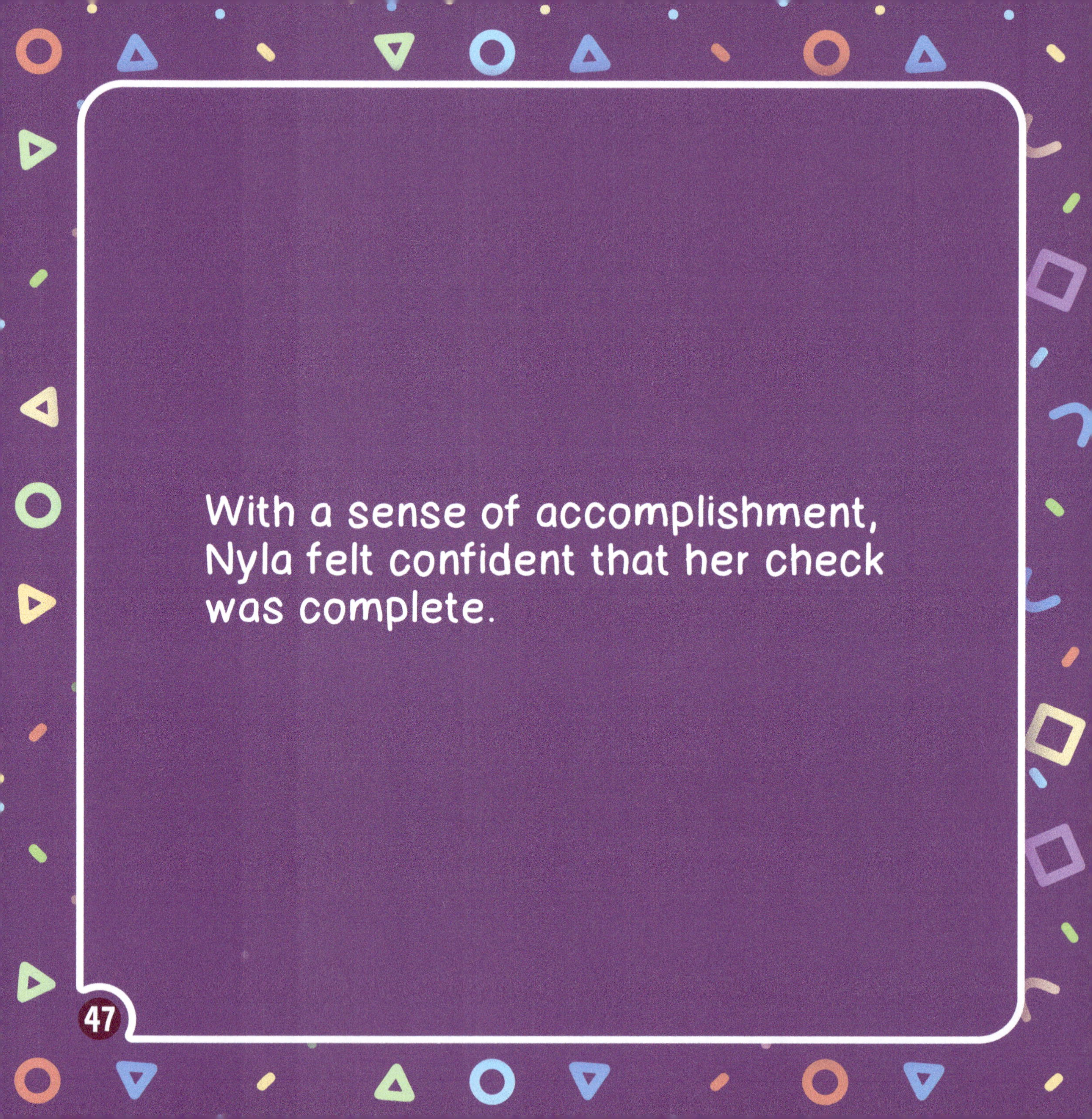

With a sense of accomplishment, Nyla felt confident that her check was complete.

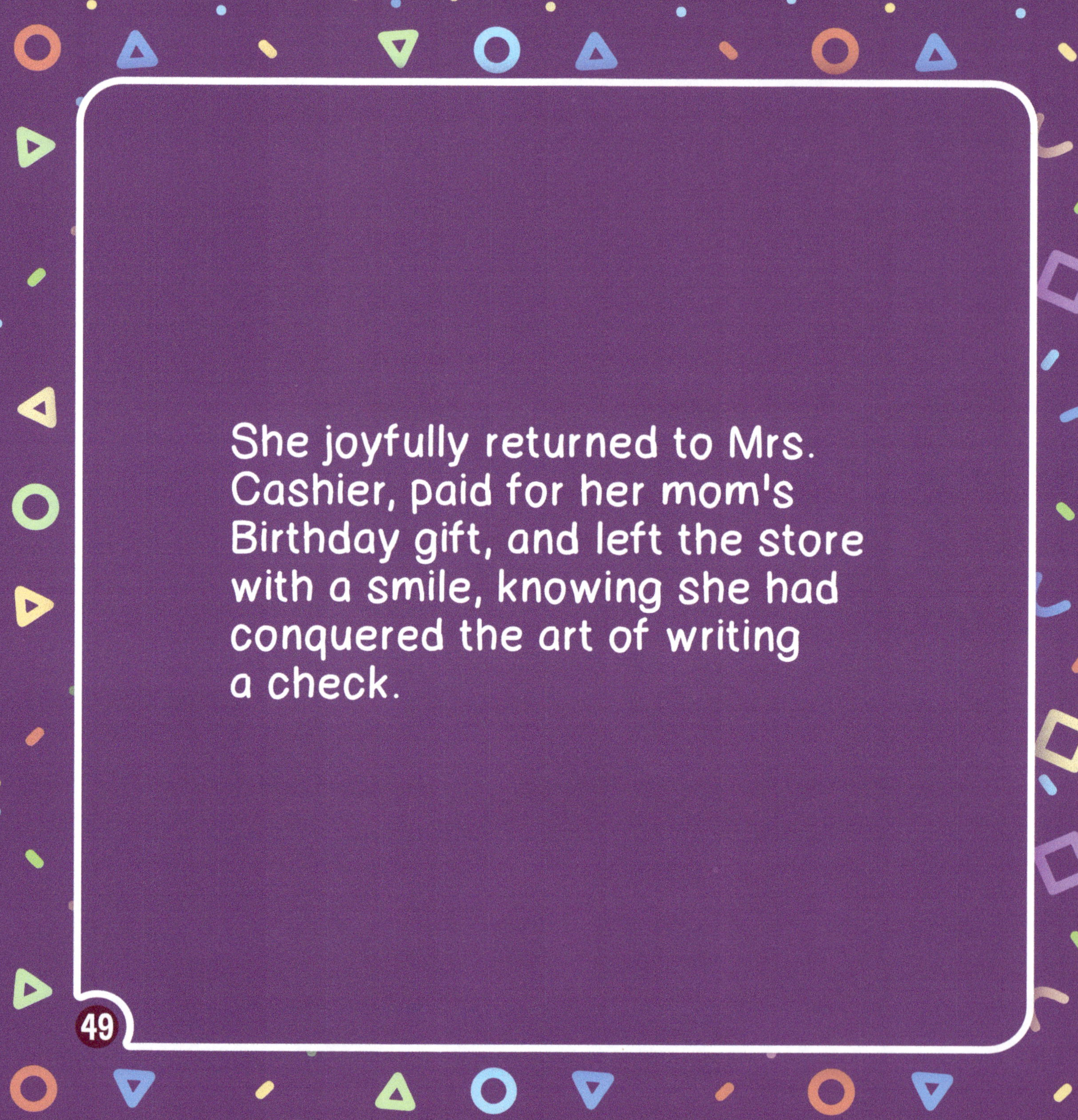

She joyfully returned to Mrs. Cashier, paid for her mom's Birthday gift, and left the store with a smile, knowing she had conquered the art of writing a check.

HAPPYBIRTHDAY
50

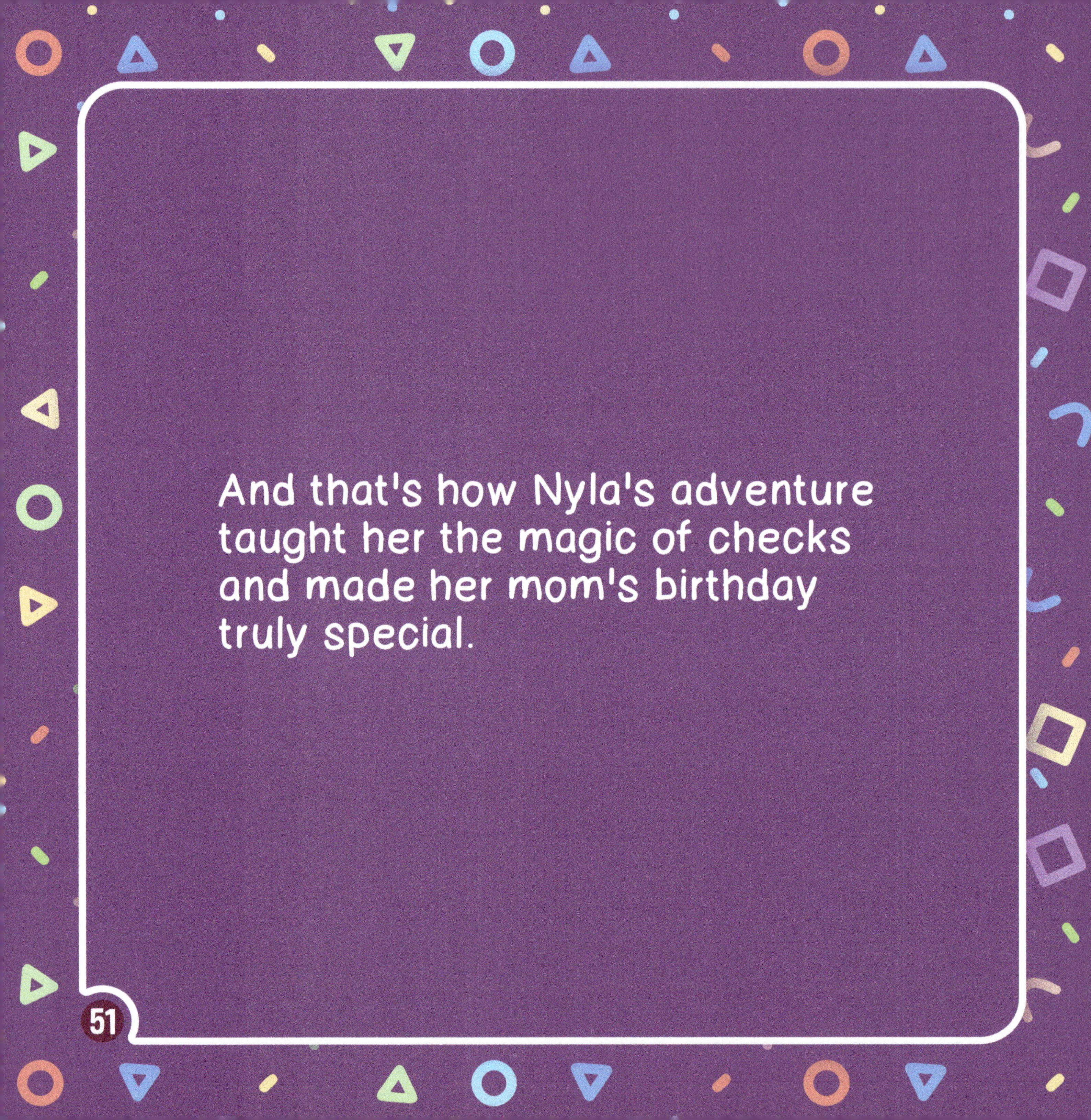

And that's how Nyla's adventure taught her the magic of checks and made her mom's birthday truly special.

The End

Sarha Simeon-Wright is the proud daughter of Haitian immigrants who has worn many hats throughout her career journey. From owning her own preschool to transitioning into home health care, she eventually found her way back to her true passion in education as a substitute teacher.

With a deep-rooted belief in the transformative power of education, Sarha has witnessed firsthand the disparities present in social classes. Motivated by a desire to make a difference, she embarked on a mission to teach financial literacy in her community and beyond.

It is with this same passion and dedication that Sarha has created this book, aiming to bridge the gaps in financial literacy and empower individuals to take control of their financial futures. As her husband, I am truly honored to watch her grow and touch the world.

Credit Chris McNish for photo.